Q is for Queen Esther

Dr. C. White-Elliott
Illustrated by Waleed Ahmad

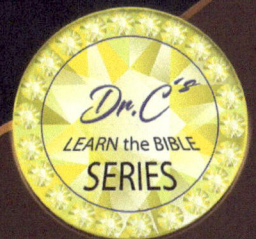

Dr. C's LEARN the BIBLE SERIES

www.clfpublishing.org
909.315.3161

Cover design by Senir Design. Contact info: info@senirdesign.com

Illustrations by Walheed Ahmad on Fivver.com.

ISBN #978-1-945102-73-8

Printed in the United States of America.

This book is dedicated to my youngest grandchild, Zuri Dior White, whom I lovingly call "Precious" because she is so very precious and also "Lil' Punkin" after my mother, who was called "Punkin" by all her grandchildren.

There was a famous king named Xerxes (whose formal name is Ahasuerus) who was searching for a queen. Young women from all around showed up, hoping they would be the new queen. After weeks and weeks of searching, a young Jewish woman named Hadassah was chosen because she was the most beautiful young maiden. Although Hadassah was her Jewish birth name, everyone called her Esther.

After Esther was chosen to be the
new queen, she dressed in a
beautiful royal gown with the help of
her royal servants. Then, she went
before her new husband, the king,
and he gave her a beautiful crown
while the royal court watched.

Not too much later, Esther's cousin Mordecai learned of an evil plot for all the Jews to be killed there in Persia. He went to Esther and told her all about it. When Esther heard the terrible news, her heart was broken. She did not want harm to come to her people. So, she had to come up with a plan of her own.

When Esther learned the king's right-hand man Haman was behind the evil plot, she put her plan into action. She decided to host a royal feast, and the only two people to be invited were her husband, the king, and Haman. That night, she told her husband about Haman's evil plot to have the Jews killed. She also revealed to her husband that she was a Jew and that her life was now in danger because of Haman's plot. Haman tried to deny what he had done. But, the king believed the word of his queen and vowed to protect her and her people. That made Esther's heart very happy.

Once Xerxes, the king, learned of the evil plot, he was able to step in and make some changes that would allow the Jews to defend themselves during battle. He also made sure the fate Haman had designed for Mordecai would be done to him: hanging from the gallows.

Eventually, war broke out between
the Jews and the Persians. The
Jews were victorious and their
lives were spared all because of the
changes the king had made after
Esther had shared with him
Haman's evil scheme.

When King Xerxes learned about Mordecai's bravery in sharing with his young cousin Esther about how the Jews would be killed, the king honored Mordecai with a special robe and ring that he wore while riding through the city upon a beautiful horse that was part of the king's herd.

After the war and the celebration of Mordecai, King Xerxes and Queen Esther and all the Jews were very happy. There was peace in the kingdom because God had prevailed and protected His people: the Jews.

www.ingramcontent.com/pod-product-compliance
Lightning Source LLC
Chambersburg PA
CBHW041956100426
42813CB00019B/2904

* 9 7 8 1 9 4 5 1 0 2 7 3 8 *